Published in 1996 by
Troddy Books
An imprint of
Regency House Publishing Limited
The Grange
Grange Yard
London SE1 3AG

ISBN 185361 438 6

Printed in Singapore

How to have fun with paper

Stewart Cowley

TRODDY BOOKS

Getting Started

Paper is a wonderful thing. It's easy to cut and fold and can be fixed with glue, staples or sticky tape. It's easy to decorate, as you can draw or paint on it, spray it with paints, or glue things onto it. It comes in many types and colours and it can be bought almost anywhere. So it doesn't matter where you are – at home, in the car, on holiday – you can always find some paper to make things with.

Here are some of the types of paper you can use:
- newspaper
- pages from a magazine
- writing paper
- gift-wrapping paper
- plain white paper, the sort used in printers and typewriters
- wallpaper – very good for making strong paper hats
- origami paper – usually sold in packs in different colours
- art paper – sometimes has bits and pieces woven into it, like leaves or gold thread, or is embossed or coloured with a pattern

Other basic things you will need:
- glue – in bottles, twist-up tubes or pens
- sticky tape
- stapler
- blunt-ended scissors
- ruler
- pencils, pens and paints
- needle and thread

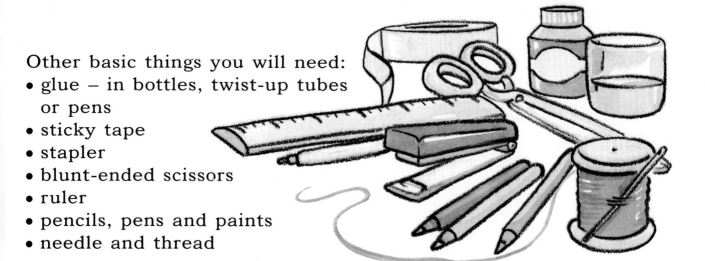

A Few Helpful Hints

If you need a perfect square, here's how to make one. Take any piece of paper, and fold one corner across diagonally, until side A meets side B. Fold over the overlap and crease. Cut off the overlap along the line.

Use blunt-ended scissors, as they are safer. Before you start, read the instructions right through to the end, and collect together everything you need.

Cover the surface you are working on with layers of newspaper, to make sure you don't scratch it or get glue or paint on it.

And always tidy up when you have finished!

1

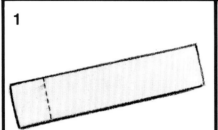

Fold over at least 5 cm at one end of the paper.

2

Turn the paper over and fold over another 5 cm. Keep folding and turning until you have a long concertina.

3

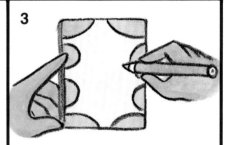

With a pencil, draw on your shape. The shape should touch the folds of the paper at both sides.

4

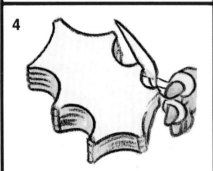

Cut out the shape, but don't cut it where it touches the folds.

5

Open out the paper, and you will have a long string of identical shapes.

6

Decorate the shapes however you like. They can all look the same, or you can make each one different.

You will need
● 1 long piece of paper, at least 10 cm high and as long as you like
● Scissors ● Pencil ● Felt-tip pens or paints to decorate

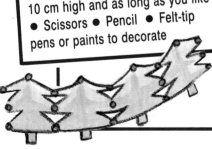

Make sure that a large part of the shape touches the folds, or that it touches them in two or three places. This will make the concertina stronger.

Of course, this doesn't have to be a Christmas

decoration – try an Easter egg, or a Hallowe'en pumpkin, or a heart for Valentine's Day.

Chain Decoration

1

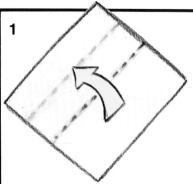

Fold both pieces of card in half and crease along the fold.

2

On one piece of card, draw two lines from the fold to the centre, about 6 cm apart.

3

Cut along these lines.

4

Fold the cut-out section to one side and crease along the fold.

5

Open the card and push the cut section in to the centre.

6

Glue the second piece of card to the back of the first.

You will need
● 2 pieces of thin card, about 20 cm square ● Ruler ● Pencil
● Felt-tip pens or paints

Decorate the outside and inside of your card with pens or paints. You could also stick on glitter or sequins, bows or buttons, to make your 3-D card more effective.

Pop-up Cards

1

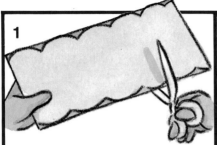

Cut a decorative pattern along the top of the paper, and along the bottom too if you like.

2

Draw a line 30 mm from the top and bottom edges. Draw lines from top to bottom 10-15 mm apart.

3

Fold the paper in half. Cut strips from the fold upwards as far as the 30 mm line.

4

Unfold the paper. Curl into a tube and glue the overlapping edges.

5

To make a handle, glue the ends of the strip of card inside the top edge of the lantern.

6

Push down gently so that the sides bulge outwards into a lantern shape.

You will need
- Rectangle of coloured paper at least 300 mm high
- Strip of thin card 30 mm wide and 200 mm long
- Ruler • Scissors • Pens or paints to decorate

To decorate your lantern, you can cut a fringe out of crêpe paper and glue them around the inside of the bottom edge.

Make lots of lanterns in different sizes and tie a loop of string or thread through the handles.

Thread a pole through the strings and hang it up. They also make good Christmas tree decorations.

Chinese Lantern

1

Trim the pictures to the nearest 10 mm in width. Label them 1, 2 and 3.

2

Lay the pictures out and cut a piece of paper to the same total length and height as the pictures.

3

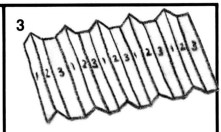

Mark the paper into 10 mm sections. Number the sections and fold the card along the lines, as shown.

4

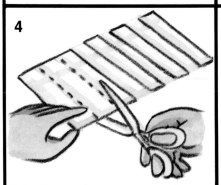

Mark each picture into 10 mm sections. Cut each picture into strips.

5

Glue the strips from picture 1 on to the section marked 1, in order.

6

Glue on the strips from pictures 2 and 3 in the same way. Stand the card up and you will see a different picture from the right, the front and the left.

You will need
● Three pictures from a magazine, trimmed to the same height and width
● Piece of thin card or stiff paper ● Scissors ● Glue
● Ruler ● Pencil

Three-Way Picture

1

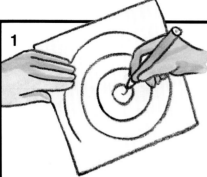

Starting from the centre, draw a spiral. Keep the space between the lines the same width.

2

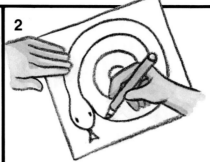

Draw a snake's head, eyes and tongue. Draw markings on the snake all the way round.

3

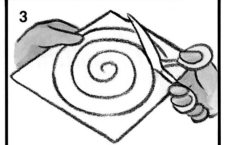

Cut around the spiral, following the line you have drawn, until you reach the centre.

4

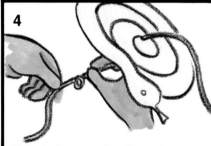

Knot the end of a piece of cotton and thread the needle. Push the needle up through the centre of the snake.

5

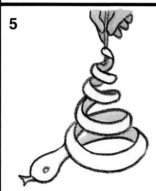

Gently pull on the thread to open up the spiral.

6

Hold the snake above a radiator or air vent, and it will revolve.

You will need
- Large square of stiff paper
- Needle and thread
- Pencil
- Pens or paints to decorate

Don't hold or hang the snake over light bulbs, fires, stoves, candles or any other source of heat, as it could catch fire.

Make several snakes, all different sizes and colours. Tie the threads to a coat hanger and hang it above a radiator. Watch them all revolve!

Spinning Snake

1

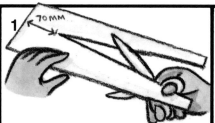

At one end of the paper, mark a point in the centre 70 mm from the end. Draw a long narrow V shape from this point to the other end.

2

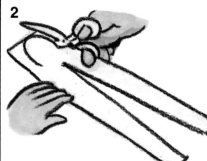

Cut out the V shape. Draw on the snake's head and cut around it.

3

At the join of the V, fold one leg over the other at a right angle.

4

Fold the second leg over the first at a right angle. Continue folding the legs over and over until there is only 50 mm left.

5

Glue the ends together to make a tail.

6

Gently pull the paper out into a snake.

You will need
- Long strip of paper about 50 mm wide ● Ruler
- Pencil

Decorate the snake with glitter or sequins. Stick on sequins for eyes.

You can use any length of paper you like – it doesn't have to be only 50 mm long.

Make a whole family of snakes in different widths, lengths and colours.

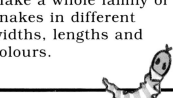

Slippery Serpent

1

Fold the paper in half, crease it and unfold. Fold all corners in the central crease.

2

Fold in half.

3

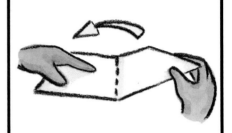

Fold in half across the middle, crease and unfold.

4

Fold up both bottom corners, so that the lower edge meets the central crease. Turn the paper over.

5

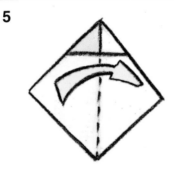

Fold it in half across the middle.

6

Hold the open end with the longest edge towards you. Bring it down sharply, and it will go bang.

You will need
• a rectangle of paper

Decorate your poppers with stars, streaks of lightning and sunbursts, or with a word such as BANG in big colourful letters.

Fill your popper with confetti or lots of tiny pieces of paper. When you pop the popper, they will fall out in a shower. (This needs a lot of clearing up!)

Party Popper

1

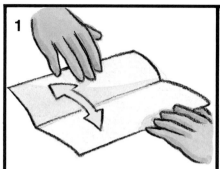

Fold the paper in half lengthways. Crease along the fold, then unfold it.

2

Fold the top corners in to the crease.

3

Fold A and B in to the crease.

4

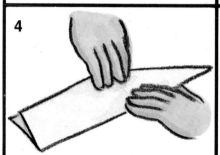

Fold the paper in half along the middle crease.

5

Fold one side down to the bottom edge. Turn the plane over and do the same on the other side. These are the wings.

6

Flatten out the wings. Hold the dart underneath – and throw it!

You will need
● A rectangle of stiff paper

Decorate the plane with a cockpit and wing markings.

To throw it, hold it in front of your shoulder and throw it gently forwards and upwards. If you fling it too hard it will nose dive!

Write a message on the paper before you start to fold it.

Paper Plane

1

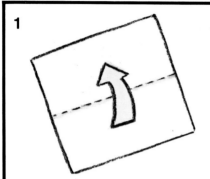

Fold the paper in half diagonally and crease along the fold.

2

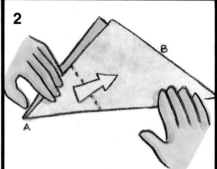

Fold A up to B and crease.

3

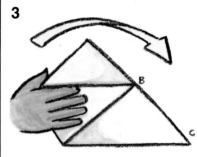

Turn the cup over from left to right.

4

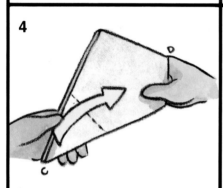

Fold C to D.

5

Fold point E towards you and tuck it in between the two layers of paper.

6

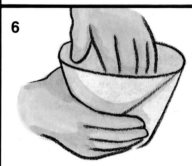

Turn the cup over and do the same on the other side. Open out the cup and pour in a cold drink.

You will need
• 1 square of paper – greaseproof paper is best

Don't pour hot drinks into this cup, as you might burn your fingers.

Take some greaseproof paper on a picnic, and impress everyone with your instant crockery!

Decorate the outside of the cup before you open it out.

Quick Paper Cup

1

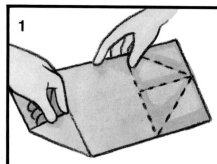

Fold the paper in half lengthways, crease and unfold. Fold the corners in to the crease.

2

Fold in half along the central crease.

3

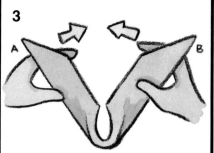

Push A and B towards each other to curve not fold. Hold A inside B.

4

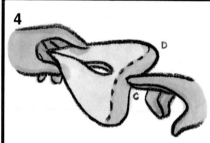

Turn the flat surface towards you, push point C up into the centre, then D and E will come together.

5

Carefully push point C to make the tail, fold out D and E. Cut out a fin from each side, as shown by the dotted line.

6

Bend the fins outwards. Paint scales, eyes and a mouth on the fish.

You will need
- Piece of paper about 200 mm x 100 mm
- Strip of paper about 150 mm x 35 mm
- Scissors.

To make the top and bottom fins

Fold the strip of paper in half. Cut each end into a curve.

With the tail towards you, pull D and E apart to flatten the fish out.

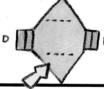

Cut two slots 40 mm long. Push the folded strip of paper through the slots. Close D and E again.

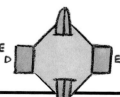

Folded Fish

1

Take a rectangle of paper at least 350 mm high. Fold it in half so the shortest edges meet. Crease along the fold.

2

Fold in half again so the shortest edges meet. Crease along the fold, then open out the paper.

3

Fold the corners down so that the top edges meet the middle crease.

4

To make the brim of the hat, fold up the lower edge on one side and crease it.

5

Turn the hat over, and do the same on the other side.

6

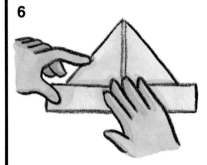

Press down along all the folds to crease them well.

You will need
- a rectangle of paper. The shorter edge should be at least 350 mm.

To make a clown's hat, stick large buttons or circles cut out of coloured paper on the front.

To make a Robin Hood hat, push the end of a feather under the brim and fix it with sticky tape or staples.

To make a summer hat, paint on flowers or stick on flower shapes cut out of coloured paper.

Paper Hat